Rounders

by Kay Livorse
illustrated by Jeff Shelly and Paul Casale

Chapters

Harcourt
Orlando Boston Dallas Chicago San Diego

Visit *The Learning Site!*
www.harcourtschool.com

The Basics of Baseball

Baseball was developed from a game called rounders. Rounders was played in England in the 1600s. In rounders, the players use a bat and ball. They score by going around the bases. English immigrants brought the game to America in the 1700s. If a fielder hit a runner with the ball, the runner was out. This was called soaking or plugging the runner. Since then, the game of rounders has become what we now call baseball.

Baseball teams did not all follow the same rules at first. Then Alexander Cartwright and some of his friends formed a team. It was called the Knickerbocker Base Ball Club of New York.

The term *Knickerbocker* came from the style of pants worn by the early Dutch settlers in New York. It has come to mean any New Yorker.

Cartwright wrote a rule book for the game in 1845. Some of his rules have been changed since then. However, baseball players today follow many of the rules Cartwright wrote.

Baseball spread throughout the nation. Early baseball players were not paid for playing. Then many clubs began to attract players by offering them a modest salary. In 1869, the Cincinnati Red Stockings decided to pay all their players. They became the first professional baseball team.

By 1900 baseball was well established. There were lots of teams. Baseball was our "national pastime." It was our country's favorite sport.

When baseball fans talk about baseball, they often use words that are special to baseball. The meanings of some of these words are obvious. Other words are understood only by baseball fans.

How many of these words do you know?

ace—A team's best starting pitcher

alley—The section of the outfield between the outfielders

around the horn—A double play going from third base to second to first

bag—A base

balk—An illegal motion by the pitcher while any runners are on base

bandbox—A small ballpark that gives hitters an advantage

bang-bang play—A play in which the base runner steps on the bag just before the ball gets there, or vice versa

basket catch—A fielder catching the ball with his glove at belt level

Bronx cheer—Booing from the crowd to show their lack of appreciation

brushback—A pitch that nearly hits a batter

bush—Amateur play or behavior that shows poor sportsmanship; also "bush league"

can of corn—An easy catch by a fielder

caught looking—A batter being called out on strikes

cellar—Last place; also "basement"

cheese—A fastball

chin music—A pitch that is high and inside

circus catch—An outstanding catch by a fielder

closer—A team's relief pitcher who finishes the game

cycle—A batter hitting a single, double, triple, and home run in one game

dinger—A home run

dish—Home plate

fungo—A ball hit to a fielder during practice; usually hit by a coach using a "fungo bat," which is longer and thinner than a regular bat

gap—See *alley*

heat—A good fastball; also "heater"

high and tight—A pitch that is up in the strike zone and close to the batter; also known as "up and in"

hill—The pitcher's mound

hit and run—The runner on base starting to run before the ball is hit

homer—A home run

hot corner—Third base

jam—To throw a pitch near the batter's hands

leather—Refers to how well a fielder plays: "He showed some leather on that play."

meatball—An easy pitch to hit

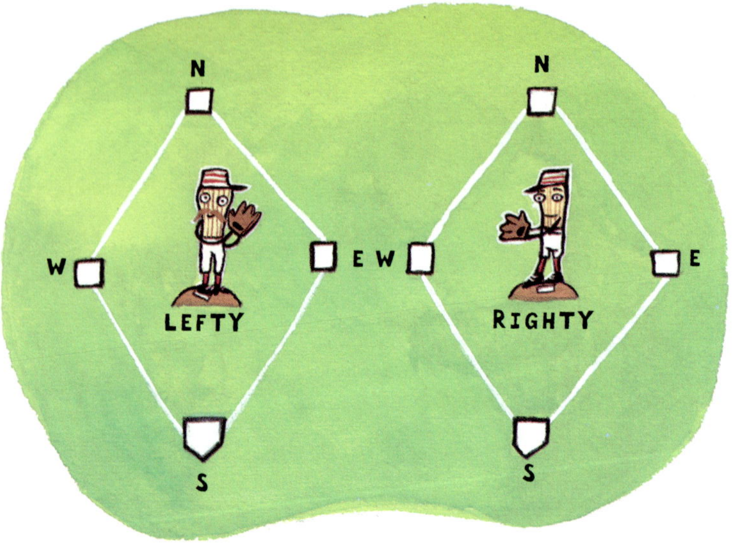

on deck—The next batter up

rhubarb—A fight or scuffle

rookie—A new player in the major leagues

rope—A hard line drive hit by a batter

rundown—A base runner getting caught between bases by the fielders

shoestring catch—A courageous, running catch made just above the fielder's shoe tops

southpaw—A left-handed pitcher

table setter—Batter whose job is to get on base for others to get him in

Texas leaguer—A hit that drops between an infielder and an outfielder

wheels—A player's legs

whiff—A strikeout

Players' Nicknames

Famous baseball players often have nicknames. Here are some you may enjoy knowing.

STAN MUSIAL

Stan "The Man" Musial played for twenty-two years, had a lifetime average of .331, and established more records during his playing days than anyone else. For sixteen consecutive years, this left-hander had a batting average of .300 or better.

LEROY PAIGE

Leroy "Satchel" Paige acquired his nickname while he was a porter at Union Station in Mobile, Alabama. He carried bags called satchels. Paige pitched for several years in the Negro Leagues and was 39 years old in his rookie year for Cleveland.

WILLIAM HENRY KEELER

This 5-foot, 4-inch player is remembered for his place-hitting abilities. "Wee Willie" Keeler said, "Keep your eye on the ball and hit 'em where they ain't." That is exactly what a place hitter does. Good grammar was not Wee Willie's strength. Hitting a baseball was. He batted .424 in 1897 while playing for the Baltimore Orioles. Wee Willie was small, but he was a big hitter.

JOE DIMAGGIO

"Joltin' Joe" DiMaggio has a certain ring to it, don't you think? His bat also had a ring to it. His best-known record was getting at least one hit in fifty-six games in a row. That hitting streak lasted for two months. DiMaggio was also known for his skill in the outfield. He played for the New York Yankees and was also called the "Yankee Clipper."

TED WILLIAMS

"The Splendid Splinter" is one of the best hitters and outfielders in major league history. In his first season, his batting average was .327. He was the first rookie to lead the league in runs batted in. He was batting champion in the American League six times. Playing for the Red Sox, he was named Most Valuable Player twice.

WILLIE MAYS

The "Say Hey Kid" was given that nickname by a sportswriter. Willie Mays greeted his fellow players with an enthusiastic "Say hey." He was an outstanding outfielder and batter for the Giants. He won the Rookie of the Year award in 1951. The "Say Hey Kid" is still one of the most famous players ever to have played the game.

WALTER JOHNSON

One of the greatest major league pitchers, Johnson was nicknamed "The Big Train" because he threw the ball so fast. With this overpowering fastball, Johnson led the American League in strikeouts twelve times. He threw 110 shutouts. In 1913, he had a 36-7 win-loss record.

BOB FELLER

"Rapid Robert" Feller was so nicknamed because of his fastball. Some think that he is the greatest right-handed pitcher of all time. So far, he is the only pitcher ever to throw a no-hitter on opening day. He was the Cleveland Indians' most valuable pitcher for years.

GEORGE HERMAN RUTH

When George Herman "Babe" Ruth first joined professional baseball, he was not yet twenty-one years old. Because he was not an adult, the owner of the Orioles, Jack Dunn, became his guardian. Other players called him "Dunn's Baby" and gave him his nickname, "The Babe."

Ruth started his professional career as a pitcher. He won 89 games for Boston in the three years he was with the team. He also won three World Series games for the Red Sox. He later became known as the "Sultan of Swat" because of his tremendous home-run hitting ability. The "Bambino" (Italian for "Babe") won ten home run crowns. He also played in seven World Series.

Did You Know That?

- Satchel Paige called his fastball his "be" ball, "because it be where I want it to be." His advice to pitchers was "throw strikes. Home plate don't move." His advice in general was, "Don't look back, something might be gaining on you."

- Lawrence "Yogi" Berra was one of the best catchers in the American League. He had a cartoon character named after him, Yogi Bear. Berra is the most quoted man in baseball, saying such things as "No wonder nobody doesn't come here, it's too crowded"; "I didn't really say all those things that I said"; and "It ain't over till it's over."

• Comedians Bud Abbott and Lou Costello are the only people not connected with baseball who are in the Baseball Hall of Fame. They achieved that honor because of their comedy routine called "Who's on First?"

• The bat that most professional baseball players use is the Louisville Slugger. Three million are made every year out of ash wood.

• A baseball cover has 108 hand-sewn stitches. One of the umpire's duties is to rub a special mud on about twelve dozen baseballs that are used in a game. The mud takes the shine off the leather and raises the grain for a better grip. The mud is gathered from a certain place on the Delaware River.

• Each team uses about 18,000 balls in a season.

center fielder
outfield
left fielder
right fielder
second base
shortstop
base path
pitcher
third base
pitcher's mound
first base
foul territory
batter
home plate
umpire
catcher